I0797632

ICONIC NATIONAL PARKS

GREAT SMOKY MOUNTAINS NATIONAL PARK

BY EMMA KAISER

Core Library

An Imprint of Abdo Publishing
abdobooks.com

Cover image: Great Smoky Mountains National Park is famous for its stunning mountain views.

abdobooks.com

Published by Abdo Publishing, a division of ABDO, PO Box 398166, Minneapolis, Minnesota 55439.

Printed in the United States of America, North Mankato, Minnesota.
052025
092025

Cover Photo: Sean Board/iStockphoto
Interior Photos: National Park Service, 4–5; Shutterstock Images, 7, 36 (clipboard), 36 (boot), 36 (trash bag), 36 (flower), 36 (fire), 36 (binoculars); Red Line Editorial, 8; KenCanning/E+/Getty Images, 10–11; Luc Novovitch/Danita Delimont/Alamy, 12; Bettmann/Getty Images, 15; Kelly VanDellen/Shutterstock Images, 18–19; Billy McDonald/Shutterstock Images, 20, 26–27, 45; iStockphoto, 23; Ben McMurtray/Shutterstock Images, 25; Cavan Images/Getty Images, 28; Carolyn Franks/Shutterstock Images, 31; Michele Burgess/Alamy, 32; Seiya Kawamoto/DigitalVision/Getty Images, 34–35; Mark Skitsky/Shutterstock Images, 36 (hands); Tom Sherlin/The Daily Times/AP Images, 40; Ali Majdfar/Moment/Getty Images, 42 (top); Francisco Blanco/Shutterstock Images, 42 (middle); Alex Grichenko/iStockphoto, 42 (bottom); Joel Carillet/iStockphoto, 43 (top); Dennis Govoni/Moment/Getty Images, 43 (middle); Sue Smith/500Px Plus/Getty Images, 43 (bottom)

Editor: Christa Kelly
Series Designer: Marley Richmond

Library of Congress Control Number: 2024949000

Publisher's Cataloging-in-Publication Data

Names: Kaiser, Emma, author.
Title: Great Smoky Mountains National Park / by Emma Kaiser
Description: Minneapolis, Minnesota: Abdo Publishing, 2026 | Series: Iconic national parks | Includes online resources and index.
Identifiers: ISBN 9781098297176 (lib. bdg.) | ISBN 9798384919698 (ebook)
Subjects: LCSH: Great Smoky Mountains National Park (N.C. and Tenn.)--Juvenile literature. | Mountain ranges--Juvenile literature. | Natural monuments--Juvenile literature. | Scenic landscapes--Juvenile literature. | National parks and reserves--Juvenile literature.
Classification: DDC 975.6--dc23

CONTENTS

CHAPTER ONE

REACHING THE SUMMIT

Kristi and her two best friends were breathing heavily as they hiked. They listened to the sound of leaves crunching under their hiking boots. They had been hiking all morning, climbing higher and higher up the trail, and now they were nearly to the summit.

For her birthday, Kristi had decided that she wanted to hike a portion of the Appalachian Trail with her friends. The Appalachian Trail is a hiking trail in

Since Great Smoky Mountains National Park opened, more than 500 million visitors have explored the park.

WHAT IS APPALACHIA?

The Blue Ridge mountain range is part of an even larger mountain system called the Appalachian Mountains. States that contain parts of this mountain system make up a region called Appalachia. The region spans about 206,000 miles (332,000 km) across 13 states. Appalachia covers all of West Virginia and parts of Alabama, Georgia, Kentucky, Maryland, Mississippi, New York, North Carolina, Ohio, Pennsylvania, South Carolina, Tennessee, and Virginia.

the eastern United States. It's more than 2,000 miles (3,200 km) long, beginning in Georgia and ending in Maine. Kristi and her friends were hiking the part of the trail that went through Great Smoky Mountains National Park in Tennessee. As they walked, they approached the state's border. Soon, they would be able to look out into North Carolina.

The trio was approaching Kuwohi. Kuwohi is the highest point in Great Smoky Mountains National Park. At 6,643 feet (2,025 m), it is also the highest

Kuwohi gives a spectacular view of the park's mountains, making it one of the most popular sites in Great Smoky Mountains National Park.

point in Tennessee. The girls left the forest trail and stepped onto a concrete ramp that would take them to the top of Kuwohi's observation tower. As they reached the top of the tower, Kristi gasped at the view. It was a clear, sunny day, and Kristi could see for miles. Below her lay miles of rolling mountains, blanketed in spruce-fir forests. She took in the wonder of the Great Smoky Mountains. It was Kristi's best birthday yet.

THE GREAT SMOKY MOUNTAINS

National parks are places that are set aside by the federal government because they are important

GREAT SMOKY MOUNTAINS NATIONAL PARK MAP

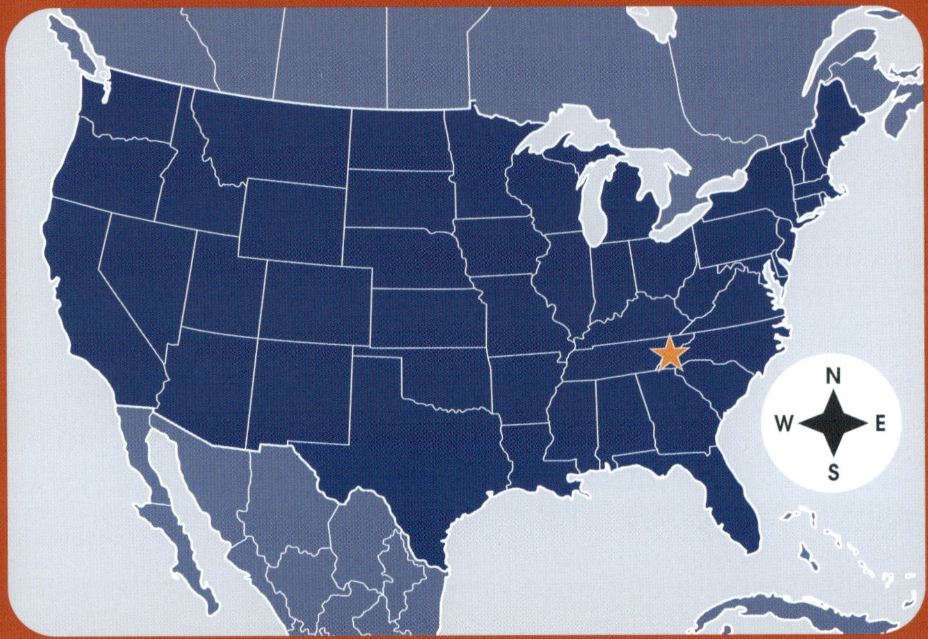

Great Smoky Mountains National Park is located in the southeastern United States. It spans across parts of Tennessee and North Carolina. Why do you think the park's geographical location makes it such a popular destination?

geographical or cultural landscapes. Great Smoky Mountains National Park is one of these sites. It is located in the southeastern United States. The park sits on the border between North Carolina and Tennessee.

Great Smoky Mountains National Park protects a portion of the Great Smoky Mountains, part of the larger Blue Ridge mountain range. The park is made up of 522,427 acres (211,400 ha). Most of this land consists of forest. In 2023, Great Smoky Mountains National Park hosted more than 13 million visitors, making it the most visited park in the United States. It has more yearly visitors than Yosemite, Yellowstone, and Grand Canyon National Parks combined. Visitors come from all over the world to hike, camp, and see the beautiful views that Great Smoky Mountains National Park has to offer.

PERSPECTIVES

A POPULAR DESTINATION

There are many reasons why Great Smoky Mountains National Park is so popular. For one, it's highly accessible. More than half the population of the United States can travel to the park in just half a day's drive or less. The park is also known for its natural beauty and impressive views. Hiking trails also crisscross through the park. Hiking tour guide Robert Hartsig says that the park has some of the best hiking trails in the country, with beautiful views of waterfalls, rivers, and the surrounding mountains.

CHAPTER TWO

HISTORY OF GREAT SMOKY MOUNTAINS NATIONAL PARK

The mountains found in Great Smoky Mountains National Park formed millions of years ago. Ancient artifacts found in the area show that humans began living in the region at least 10,000 years ago.

The Great Smoky Mountains got their name from the native Cherokee people. These people have lived in the region for thousands of years. The Cherokee call the mountains The Place of Blue Smoke because of the mist that

The Great Smoky Mountains are among the oldest mountains on Earth.

Today, the Cherokee Nation has more than 450,000 members.

floats above the peaks. This mist is caused by fog rising from the region's forests.

CONFLICT FOR LAND

European settlers moved into the area in the late 1700s. They settled on land that still belonged to the Cherokee Nation. This caused conflict between the two groups. In 1838, the US government forced all members of the Cherokee Nation to leave their homes and travel west. Soldiers marched more than 15,000 Cherokee people from their homes near the Smoky Mountains to unfamiliar areas of Arkansas and Oklahoma. The march took six months. Many had to walk most of the 1,200-mile (2,000 km) journey. More than 4,000 Cherokee people died from starvation, cold, and disease

CHEROKEE NATION TODAY

About 11,000 members of the Cherokee Nation still live near the Great Smoky Mountains. Many live on the Cherokee Indian Reservation, which covers five counties in western North Carolina. Many members of the Cherokee Nation still pass their history and traditions along to younger generations. The Great Smoky Mountains remain a sacred area to many members of the Cherokee Nation.

during the long walk. Today, this forced removal is known as the Trail of Tears.

After the removal of the Cherokee Nation, more white settlers began moving into the area. Small, isolated towns grew into larger communities. By the 1900s, much of the land was used for farming. Other parts were bought by timber and paper companies. The companies cut down much of the forests. People began to worry about protecting the area around the Great Smoky Mountains. They began thinking about ways to preserve it for future generations.

FORMING A NATIONAL PARK

Some national parks were easier to form in the United States than others. For example, Yellowstone National Park consists of land that was already owned by the US government. This meant that the government could easily make the land a national park. But the area that now makes up Great Smoky Mountains National Park was owned by hundreds of individual people

Calvin Coolidge served as president from 1923 to 1929.

and companies. In 1926, President Calvin Coolidge signed a bill that declared the Great Smoky Mountains a national park. But it would take many years to raise enough money to purchase the land.

The park would include land from Tennessee and North Carolina. The two states donated a combined 300,000 acres (120,000 ha) of land. Roughly 150,000 additional acres (61,000 ha) had to be purchased from individuals who owned property in the designated park area. Conservationists, ordinary citizens, and even schoolchildren raised $10 million to purchase the remaining land and establish the park.

A group called the Civilian Conservation Corps helped develop the land for the park. They created trails, built roads and bridges, and established campgrounds for visitors. The park officially opened in September 1940. President Franklin D. Roosevelt gave a speech commemorating the park at a spot called the Newfound Gap. Great Smoky Mountains National Park was officially open for visitors.

PERSPECTIVES

LEAVING HOME

Not everyone was happy about the Smoky Mountains becoming a national park. When the park was created, nearly 6,000 people were forced to move off the park's land. Many people had to give up their homes and farms, including families who had lived in the area for generations. Some elderly people were allowed to live out the rest of their lives in the park. Others were granted short-term leases, which allowed them to stay in the area temporarily.

STRAIGHT TO THE **SOURCE**

President Franklin D. Roosevelt addressed the public at Great Smoky Mountains National Park's dedication ceremony. He said:

> ***Here in the Great Smokies, we have come together to dedicate these mountains, streams, and forests to the service of the millions of American people. We are living under governments which are proving their devotion to national parks. . . . There are trees here that stood before our forefathers came to this continent; there are brooks that will run as clear as on the day the first pioneer cupped his hand and drank from them. In this park, we shall conserve . . . the pine, the redbud, the dogwood, the azalea, the rhododendron, the trout, and the thrush for the happiness of the American people.***

Source: Franklin D. Roosevelt. "Address at Dedication of Great Smoky Mountains National Park." ***American Presidency Project*****, n.d., presidency.ucsb.edu. Accessed 12 Aug. 2024.**

CONSIDER YOUR AUDIENCE

Adapt this passage for a different audience, such as your family or friends. Write a blog post conveying this same information for the new audience. How does your post differ from the original text and why?

CHAPTER THREE

PLANTS AND ANIMALS

Great Smoky Mountains National Park is the most biologically diverse national park in the United States. More than 20,000 different documented species of organisms can be found in the park. These species thrive in the park's temperate climate.

The Great Smoky Mountains' unique climate plays a large role in its biological diversity. The park receives anywhere from 55 to 85 inches (140–220 cm) of rain each year.

Scientists estimate that there are thousands of undiscovered species living in Great Smoky Mountains National Park.

Great Smoky Mountains National Park is home to more flowering plants than any other US national park.

This heavy rain helps many different types of vegetation thrive. The Great Smoky Mountains themselves also shape the area's diversity. The mountains provide a range of habitats at different altitudes. Some species prefer higher altitudes, while others thrive in the lower altitudes of the lowlands. The mountains provide ideal habitats for all of these species.

DIVERSE FORESTS

Nearly 95 percent of Great Smoky Mountains National Park is covered in forests. One-quarter of these forests are old-growth forests. *Old-growth* means that the forests consist of trees that have had hundreds of years to mature without being logged or disturbed. About 100 species of native trees are found in the park, along with more than 1,500 species of flowering plants.

There are four main types of forests found in the park. These forests include spruce-fir forests, northern hardwood forests, hemlock forests, and pine and oak forests. Spruce-fir forests grow at the highest elevations. They are found at about 4,500 feet (1,400 m) above sea level.

Northern hardwood forests grow in the middle to upper elevations of the park. These forests consist of maple, beech, and birch trees, which create beautiful fall colors. Hemlock forests grow in sandy, shady areas, while pine and oak forests grow best in sloping areas where the soil drains quickly. These diverse forests offer habitats for many different animals within the park.

WETLANDS

Wetlands make up less than 1 percent of the total land area within Great Smoky Mountains National Park. However, more than 25 percent of plant species found in the park rely on wetland ecosystems. Wetlands serve many important roles, including controlling flooding, protecting groundwater, and preventing erosion caused by streams. Many animals within the park also rely on wetland habitats. These animals include amphibians, insects, birds, and fish.

ANIMALS OF THE PARK

The Great Smoky Mountains are a refuge for many diverse species of animals. White-tailed deer leap through the park's forests, while Indiana bats flit across the night sky. In the streams, eastern box turtles and crayfish search for food, while owls watch overhead. Many more animals call the park home, including 200 species of birds, 67 species of fish, 65 species of mammals, and 39 species of reptiles. The park also provides habitats

People should stay at least 75 feet (23 m) away from deer and elk and 300 feet (90 m) away from bears.

for 43 species of amphibians. Thirty of these species are salamanders, earning the park the title Salamander Capital of the World. The park also has a record number of mollusk and millipede species.

Great Smoky Mountains National Park contains about 2,900 miles (4,700 km) of streams. About 800 miles (1,300 km) of these waterways are home to fish. Areas of lower elevation with slower and warmer water are especially great for aquatic diversity. Some of the fish within the park's waterways are endangered. These species include the brook trout, the yellowfin

PERSPECTIVES

BEAR SAFETY

Sometimes black bears can be aggressive toward humans. In 2021, a teenage girl at Great Smoky Mountains National Park was attacked by a bear while resting in a hammock. In 2020, a hiker was killed by a bear in the park. However, the Tennessee Wildlife Resources Agency says that these tragedies are rare. It says, "Black bears are normally very elusive and shy animals . . . and unless they have become accustomed to human food sources, they tend to avoid people." Park visitors can protect themselves from bear attacks by practicing bear safety. Tourists should never leave food out for bears to find. They should also keep their distance. It is illegal to get within 50 yards (46 m) of a bear within a national park.

madtom, and the duskytail darter.

One of the most famous animals in the park is the American black bear. Some people consider this bear to be a symbol of the park. The park goes to great lengths to protect the species. Great Smoky Mountains National Park provides the largest protected area of bear habitat in the eastern United States. Scientists estimate that about 1,900 bears live in the park. This means

Black bear cubs live with their mothers for about 18 months.

there are about two bears per square mile (2.5 sq km). Bears live in all elevation levels within the park and are sometimes spotted with cubs in the spring and summer months.

EXPLORE ONLINE

Chapter Three explores the diversity of plant and animal species in the park. The video at the website below goes into more depth on this topic. How is the information from the website the same as the information in Chapter Three? What new information did you learn?

NATURE AND SCIENCE

abdocorelibrary.com/great-smoky-mountains-national-park

CHAPTER FOUR

RECREATION

There's no shortage of things to do in Great Smoky Mountains National Park. One of the main reasons people visit is to take in the sights. The park is filled with spectacular views of mountains and woodland landscapes.

There are also 90 historic structures in the park, including churches, schools, and homes. These structures show what it would have looked like to live in mountain homesteads before the park was created.

Entering Great Smoky Mountains National Park is free.

In the 1800s, overhunting and habitat loss drove the elk in Great Smoky Mountains National Park to extinction. Rangers reintroduced elk to the park in 2001.

The park's beautiful plant life is also a draw for visitors. The park is often called Wildflower National Park due to the wildflowers that bloom year-round. The park even offers trails called Wildflower Walks that are specifically chosen for wildflower viewing.

Others are drawn to Great Smoky Mountains National Park to view the park's animals. Bird-watchers search for the park's owls and warblers, while hikers hope to catch glimpses of the park's elk herds.

Those looking for animals are advised to seek out open areas such as Cades Cove. Roaring Fork Motor Nature Trail is another popular place to spot deer, elk, black bears, raccoons, turkeys, and other wild animals.

PERSPECTIVES

SOMETHING FOR EVERYONE

According to Emily Davis, a former park ranger and public affairs specialist for the park, the beauty of the Great Smoky Mountains is that there's something everyone will love. She says, "Some people come to see wildflowers and wildlife, some want to challenge themselves on a new trail, some like exploring the park's history, and some want to take a scenic drive." Whatever people's interest, the park offers a wide range of activities.

HIKING AND CAMPING

Hiking and camping are among the best ways to see Great Smoky Mountains National Park up close. There are more than 800 miles (1,300 km) of hiking trails throughout the park. The trails take hikers to caves, bluffs, and old-growth forests, all while providing beautiful

RAINBOW FALLS

One of the most popular trails in Great Smoky Mountains National Park is the hike to Rainbow Falls. This is a 5.6-mile (9 km) hike to a famous waterfall. Standing nearly 80 feet (20 m) tall, the waterfall is named for the misty rainbow that can be seen at the falls' base on sunny days. The trail includes 1,500 feet (500 m) of elevation gain with views of old-growth forest. In the summer, many hikers cool off at the falls. In the autumn, the hike offers gorgeous views of the forest's colorful foliage.

views of the Great Smoky Mountains.

Each season offers something new for hikers. Spring is the best time to view wildflowers, while summer is a great time to hike to waterfalls. Autumn offers changing colors, and winter allows hikers to see views that are normally blocked by leaves and vegetation.

Camping allows visitors to stay in the park overnight. The park offers several types of campsites. Frontcountry campsites are among the most popular options. These sites are easily accessible by car. Visitors can reserve a site for a tent, camper, or recreational

Great Smoky Mountains National Park has ten frontcountry campgrounds for visitors to choose from.

vehicle (RV). These campgrounds have restrooms, running water, and firepits. Those who want to hike to their site can reserve a backcountry campsite. These sites may be several miles away from the rest of the campgrounds. Visitors must carry their supplies with them. Group campgrounds are larger campsites for big groups of people. There are also campsites for visitors with horses.

Horseback rides are available for people of all skill levels.

PARK ACTIVITIES

There are many activities visitors can enjoy while in Great Smoky Mountains National Park. Some people come to the park to fish. The park is also popular with cyclists. Many of the roads in the park can be traveled by bicycle. Cades Cove Loop Road is one of the park's most popular bike routes. The 11-mile (18 km) road offers great views of wildlife. Several trails also allow bicycles. Those who don't bring a bicycle can rent one from the park campground.

Horseback riding is another popular activity. It's also a great way to see the park. More than 550 miles (890 km) of trails are open to horseback riders. Visitors can bring their own horses into the park, or they can take guided horseback rides. Guided rides are offered from three riding stables within the park. Horse-drawn carriage and wagon rides are also available for visitors.

FURTHER EVIDENCE

Chapter Four discusses some of the sights and activities that visitors like to enjoy in the park. What was one of the main points of this chapter? What key evidence supports this point? Read the article on the website below. Does the information on the website support this point? Or does it present new evidence?

THINGS TO DO

abdocorelibrary.com/great-smoky-mountains-national-park

CHAPTER FIVE

CARING FOR THE PARK

Everyone has a role to play in caring for Great Smoky Mountains National Park. Because so many people visit the park every year, rangers face unique challenges in keeping the landscape healthy. Bigger crowds increase the risk of damage and destruction to the park. Large numbers of people often mean more trash, more traffic interrupting wildlife crossings, and more trampling of vegetation.

More people are visiting the Smoky Mountains than ever before. From 2013 to 2023, the park saw a 42 percent increase in visitors.

LEAVE NO TRACE SEVEN PRINCIPLES

1. Plan ahead and prepare.

2. Travel and camp on durable surfaces.

3. Dispose of waste properly.

4. Leave what you find.

5. Minimize campfire impacts.

6. Respect wildlife.

7. Be considerate of other visitors.

The National Park System recommends that all visitors follow the Leave No Trace Seven Principles. Why do you think these principles matter? How does each principle protect the park and its visitors?

Visitors can help protect the park by following the Leave No Trace Seven Principles. These principles are promoted by the National Park Service. They encourage people to be conscious of their surroundings and their impact on natural areas. Some of the Leave No Trace Seven Principles include planning ahead for visits, being considerate of other visitors, and not damaging or altering the landscape. One of the most important principles requires guests to leave what they find in the park. This means leaving plants, animals, and other natural objects where they are. However, guests should never leave food, garbage, or personal belongings in the park.

STOPPING INVASIVE SPECIES

Species that are not native to an area and can cause damage to an ecosystem are called invasive species. Invasive species are often transported by humans. There are several steps park visitors can take to prevent the spread of invasive species. Visitors should buy and burn firewood within the park rather than bringing their own. They should also clean all gear and boots before entering and leaving parks. Visitors with boats should clean, drain, and dry boats and equipment before entering or leaving waterways.

PERSPECTIVES

VOLUNTEERING

While the park employs people year-round, volunteers also play a big role in preserving the park. Some volunteers give their time for a single day, while others might volunteer for a season or longer. Volunteers can help with jobs such as maintaining trails, installing park features, and serving as campground hosts. According to the National Park Service, "Volunteers need to be able to hike at least 3 miles (5 km) and safely perform strenuous and often difficult manual labor." They also should be comfortable using axes, rakes, and shovels. These tools are often used to maintain trails.

FIRE MANAGEMENT

Fire management is one of the ways scientists keep the Great Smoky Mountains healthy. Fire is a natural force that can be incredibly damaging to ecosystems. However, some ecosystems need fire to flourish.

Wildfires that humans start are especially harmful to nature and property. In November 2016, a terrible wildfire swept through the park. It eventually spread to the nearby town of Gatlinburg, Tennessee. The fire raged for nearly three weeks and burned 17,900 acres (7,200 ha). More than 14,000 people had to be evacuated. By the time the fire was controlled, 2,400 buildings were damaged, and 14 people were killed. It was one of the largest natural disasters in the state's history.

However, fire is needed to maintain healthy and sustainable ecosystems. Many species depend on fire. For example, some species of pine trees produce pine cones that open only when exposed to fire. Without fire, the pine cones won't open and their seeds can't be spread. This affects species that depend on pine trees.

Naturally occurring fires caused by lightning strikes happen about twice a year in the park. For years, rangers tried to extinguish all fires. This practice has since changed. Today, park rangers allow many natural wildfires to burn as long as they don't threaten people or property. Rangers sometimes even start controlled burns in places that benefit from fire exposure. This allows fire to benefit habitats in

Controlled burns keep the land healthy and get rid of dried plant material that could fuel unintentional fires.

controlled settings. By understanding what species and ecosystems need to thrive, humans can play an important part in protecting natural spaces.

STRAIGHT TO THE
SOURCE

Daniel "Boone" Vandzura became the chief park ranger at Great Smoky Mountains National Park in 2023. He said this about working in the park:

> ***Me and my family, we're mountain people. We liked to hunt, hike, and camp, and we love the mountains, whether it's being out on the trail and being along the streams or looking at the wildland flowers or the wildlife. Our happy spot is being in the mountains, and I'm excited to be back here. It's a wonderful location, just rich history and culture. . . . Whether it's the leaf season in the fall, whether it's fireflies, whether it's search and rescues, whether it's spring and the bears being out, every day is different, and that's a wonderful aspect of the job.***

Source: Holly Kays. "A Conversation with Smokies Chief Ranger." *Smoky Mountain Living Magazine*, 25 Mar. 2024, smliv.com. Accessed 12 Aug. 2024.

WHAT'S THE BIG IDEA?

Take a close look at this passage. What is the main connection the park ranger is making about the mountains and his job? What about these connections adds value to the job of chief park ranger?

PARK LANDMARKS

Kuwohi is the highest point in the park. It sits along the state border between Tennessee and North Carolina.

Rainbow Falls is a popular hiking destination. Visitors can often see a rainbow at the base of the falls.

Charlies Bunion is a unique rock formation that offers scenic views overlooking the park.

Mount LeConte is a popular hiking destination and the third-tallest peak in the park.

Cades Cove is a scenic valley surrounded by mountains on all sides.

Newfound Gap is a mountain pass that cuts through the park.

STOP AND THINK

Surprise Me

Chapter Two describes the early history of Great Smoky Mountains National Park. After reading this book, what two or three facts about the park's early history surprised you? Write a few sentences about each fact. Why did you find each fact surprising?

Dig Deeper

After reading this book, what questions do you still have about the Great Smoky Mountains? With an adult's help, find a few reliable sources that can help you answer your questions. Write a paragraph about what you learned.

Say What?

Studying national parks can mean learning a lot of new vocabulary. Find five words in this book you've never heard before. Use a dictionary to find out what they mean. Then write the meanings in your own words, and use each word in a new sentence.

You Are There

This book discusses several kinds of recreation that are popular in the park. Imagine you are visiting the park. Write a letter home telling your friends what activities you participated in and what you saw. Be sure to add plenty of details to your letter.

GLOSSARY

altitude
height above sea level

backcountry
wilderness

biologically diverse
hosting a variety of different species

commemorate
to celebrate or show respect for something

conservationist
a person who supports conservation, the protection of animals, plants, and natural resources

ecosystem
a community of organisms living together and interacting

erosion
the gradual wearing away of land by external forces, such as wind or water

habitat
the natural home of a plant or animal

organism
a living thing

temperate
having mild temperatures

vegetation
plants found in a particular habitat

ONLINE RESOURCES

To learn more about Great Smoky Mountains National Park, visit our free resource websites below.

Visit **abdocorelibrary.com** or scan this QR code for free Common Core resources for teachers and students, including vetted activities, multimedia, and booklinks, for deeper subject comprehension.

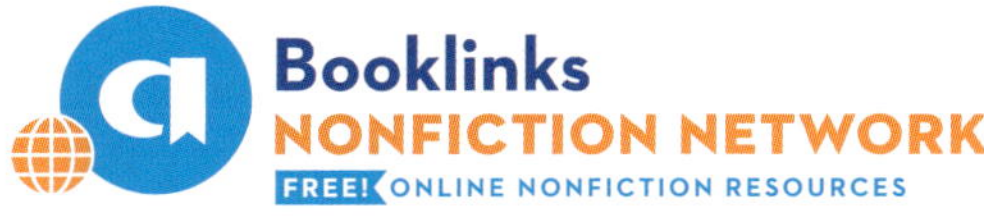

Visit **abdobooklinks.com** or scan this QR code for free additional online weblinks for further learning. These links are routinely monitored and updated to provide the most current information available.

LEARN MORE

Hulick, Kathryn. *Camping and Hiking Encyclopedia*. Abdo, 2024.

Ward, Alexa. *America's National Parks*. Lonely Planet, 2024.

INDEX

About the Author

Emma Kaiser is a writer and educator based in western Minnesota. She has a Master of Fine Arts in creative writing from the University of Minnesota, and her writing has appeared in a number of magazines and publications. She is the author of several other nonfiction books for students.